BAD INFLUENCE OF INTERNET ON KIDS

PAKEEZA KHATUN

Contents

Contents

Acknowledgements

First and foremost, we would like to thank the Almighty for the reason we are here today.

We thank every single soul who helped us to bring this anthology a successful one.

We thank Kashish Publications for giving us an opportunity and also for their constant support till the completion of the project.

Disclaimer

"Bad Influence of Internet on Kids" is totally a work of experience as well as fiction and the imaginations of our co-authors. All the thoughts, writings has been penned by the imaginative purpose of the writers itself. We do not take any responsibilities in case of plagiarism of content found as neither of publication or the compilers would be responsible for this. The co-authors will be the sole responsible of the above same.

About Us

Kashish Publications is a growing platform for all the budding writers to fulfill their dream. It is founded by Kashish Soni,a budding writer who believe that writing is the magic to heal one's heart.

"*YOU DREAM, WE ACCOMPLISHED!*"

You can contact us for solo publishing or for compiling a one of our own.

Instagram id- @kashish_publications

Gmail- sonikashish004@gmail.com

About The Project Head

He is Mr. Krishna K. Bagdi.

He hails from Madhya Pradesh. He is an entrepreneur and a digital business consultant.

He is founder of Dream World Publication DWP Writing castle and Helping Hand Foundation

He has a keen interest in writing and photography. "When you have fire of dreams in your eyes, I am serving you all here so that each writer would be appreciated when Someone reads a book.

About The Compiler

Pakeeza Khatun

Pakeeza Khatun is a writer and poet, who is also good daily life observer, depicting most of her writings about passionate love, inspiration and heartbreak. She has taken part in many anthologies. Born and raised up in Assam, recently she has won the award of The Best Writer Of 2021.

Co-author's Desk

1. Arpita Saxena

Hi myself Arpita I'm teacher by profession and loves to read novels and fond of content writing.

EDUCATION SYSTEM AND STANDARDS INDIA

Education is an important ingredient in our lives as we know the value of it. Education, the way of respect. Education, the way of honour. Education, the way of success. To be frank, in our nation (india) education system and standards are very low compared to other nations. Education is in one way in corporate schools and colleges, and in the other way in normal town schools/colleges. It's a huge disappointment that, it's affecting our development. Caste wise registrations should be neglected. Due to caste reservations, students are not able to compete each other in competitive exams. As long as the caste reservations and low standards would come to an end, India will be remained as a developing nation.

2. Anusha Sathia

Anusha is a writer and a poet hailing from India. She is currently in high school. She has been writing since quite a few years and that has been her passion. She uses her positive attitude and tireless energy to encourage others to work hard and succeed and she writes because she enjoys expressing herself. For more of her work, please check out her Instagram handle: @_thelittletherapist

Internet

The internet, has affected children's communication negatively. Over dependence on the internet has made the children abandon the traditional face to face interactions. It has led to strained relationships with their families, friends and consequently, has led to difficult communication even in their schools due to stunted development. Children who spend most of their time in the virtual world gradually withdraw from the real world. They soon become dependent on the internet to feel upbeat, accepted, and heard. And, when they are unable to access the Internet, they start experiencing anxiety, sadness, and depression. Teens use the internet to do a lot of things like searching for information, corresponding, paying bills, and doing financial transactions.

However, in the case of internet addicts, they spend most of their time engaged in browsing, chatting or gaming, instead of doing what they are actually supposed to do. Also, they are unable to keep track of the time they spend doing such activities. As a result, they lose track of time in the real world. Their studies and routine schedules are neglected. As a parent, you can surely exercise control over your child's excessive internet usage, for the sake of their physical and mental health. And, if you suspect that your teen is an internet addict or is on his way to becoming one, do seek help from a counsellor or a psychologist at the earliest.

3. Nilanjasha Howlader

She is the Nilanjasha Howlader. She is a teen of 16. She is from Kolkata, India. She is a beautiful blooming writer and a Compiler too. Till now she had compiled four anthologies i.e. Unsung Tales Estoric Minds, Scribbled Stygian Lanes and Midnight Anecdotes. She had worked in more than 100+ anthologies as a Co-author. Apart from writing, she is also a painter and she tries to paint her fantasies and tries to exaggerate her thoughts on her canvas. She had been trained in classical musicand Bharatanatyam. She also has huge interest in sports, she was also trained in Lawn tennis.

Technism!

Instead of bringing us close ,
It created a distance ,
Connected us with fake smiles,
Parted our hearts and brains.
The mind turned into a spongy thing ,
Which squeezes out nonsense when squeezed , We developed techs to help humans,
Not to transform the mankind into humanoid beings . The web has evils ,
Evils that are toxic than those societal mindsets , In the idea of exploring world at finger tips, It destroyed lives in its ways,
The web evils had contaminated the generation , Made them lifeless anatomies .

All day we gaze and gaze,
Gaze at the bright illuminated screens,
And feed upon the radio waves ,
No more we have interest in invading realism .
And soon the era will mark its end ,
Which will end up with humanoid robots with fragile brains , The existence of humans ,
Will be a myth then,
Tell us what to do ?
To continue and make the world,
Believe our existence ?!

4. KESHAR AGRE

I am keshar from, ujjain.
I am student in government engineering collage, ujjain. This is my first write.

BAD INFLUENCE OF INTERNET:-
Social media This is the world where humans have kept a different world by hiding their reality, it sees the same people which is not true, they do not worry at all about what effect this will have on the people Whether it is good or bad, he is unaware of this, and here some people are becoming influencers to influence people and then those people also call themselves influencers who do not even know the meaning of influencer themselves.
The less knowledge and depleted intellect of these people is adding a different smell to this world, the smell of western culture, the smell of self-destruction! Our country has always been known all over the world for Vedas, Puranas and its own different culture, but now a different passion has prevailed in this understanding, now you can call it hobby or madness and in this madness, people like this. They have become so blind that they cannot see anything good or bad. For just a few pennies, wrong advice is recognized in people and goes out on the wrong Sikh days, even knowing that it is all wrong. They work by forgetting their culture and rites, they do not mean anything from good to bad.

They have created such a toxic empire which is slowly spoiling our civilized society, due to all these things our young generation is being given wrong education, we have to understand this, otherwise that day. Not far away when every child of the country will start calling himself an influencer. Now what is wrong to call them too, because of these mistakes our culture is going to the trough and going towards destruction.

5. Adeela Shaikh

Adeela Shaikh is an intermediate student at SSG, Aligarh Muslim University . Born in UP and currently live in Mau(Uttar Pradesh). She is studious and natural learner. She is always more mature than the other students at school. She is a strong believer in the power of positive thinking. She is passionate towards reading since childhood. Thus keen interest in book has turned her into innovative and creative writer. Her good number of short stories and poem has been published at different sources.

Today, she is an aspiring IAS and dreamer of world famous storyteller.

Internet ka Bura Prabhav Bacchon Par

internet yuva logon ke lie ek doosare ke saath sanvaad karane, khud ko vyakt karane aur sabhee prakaar kee saamagree saajha karane ke lie tejee se vikasit hone vaala manch hai. isane ek nae saanskrtik pratimaan ko janm diya hai jo logon ke sampark ke tareeke ko badalate hue praudyogikee aur vyavasaayon ko sanchaalit karata hai. ek upakaran ke roop mein, intaranet ek dodhaaree talavaar hai. jabaki isake kaee phaayade hain, yah yuvaon ke saath saath bachchon ko bhee asvasth tareeke se bhee prabhaavit karata hai. haal ke dinon mein terah varsh se kam aayu ke aadhunik bachchon mein intaranet ka upayog badha hai. saalaana tees miliyan se adhik bachche onalain saiton par jaate hain, jisase yah intaranet par nirbhar sabase bada samooh ban jaata hai. intaranet ka upayog gharon, skoolon, pustakaalayon aur skoolon ka ek kendreey hissa ban gaya hai. intaranet par atyadhik nirbharata se vyakti ke jeevan mein phaayade aur nukasaan donon hain. intaranet ka upayog karane vaale bachche aamataur par lambe samay tak baithe rahate hain. isase motaapa badhane aur aankhon kee roshanee kam hone se unakee sehat par asar padata hai. kampyootar ke saamane lambe samay tak baithane se shaareerik gatividhi ka samay kam ho jaata hai aur ve baahar nahin khel paate hain. yah chhaatron ko hamesha apane kamaron mein band karake aur is tarah unake saamaajik sambandhon ko dheela karake khud ko baakee duniya se alag kar sakata hai. yah shodh kiya gaya hai ki intaranet ka bachchon par nakaaraatmak aur sakaaraatmak donon prabhaav padata hai. intaranet aur bachchon par kaaver es, robart ee, petreesiya em, gaileree je aur kolet bee ke anusaar, kampyootar ka upayog laabh se adhik nukasaan ka hai. bachchon ke lie yah jaanana achchha hai ki shaikshik uddeshyon ke lie kampyootar ka upayog kaise kiya jaata hai, jisamen sarphing shaikshik lekh aur skool ka homavark shaamil ho sakata hai. bachchon ke ghar ke kampyootar tak pahunch na hone ka prabhaav bachchon ke maata-pita ke vyaktitv ke aadhaar par bhinn ho sakata hai. kuchh maata-pita ghar ke kampyootar ka upayog nahin karana chaahate hain ya apane bachchon ko kampyootar tak pahunchane kee anumati nahin dena chaahate hain. aisa isalie hai kyonki unaka maanana hai ki yah achchhe se jyaada nukasaan karega. jabaki doosaron ka maanana hai ki achchhe shaikshik laabh hain. kampyootar ke upayog ke bina bachchon ka saamana karane ka tareeka bhinn hota hai. kuchh bachche soshal meediya samaaj mein khud ko akela mahasoos kar sakate hain. adhyayan se pata chalata hai ki, jin bachchon ke paas ghareloo kampyootar tak pahunch hai, unake paas achchhee shaikshik prshthabhoomi hone kee adhik sambhaavana hai jo "padhane, ganit, vyaakaran, kampyootar gyaan mein akaadamik pradarshan mein pragati aur skool pareeksha mein uchch skor se sambandhit hai, un bachchon kee tulana mein jo nahin karate hain kampyootar tak pahunch hai". haalaanki, aisee nakaaraatmak vebasaiten bhee hain jo bachchon ko intaranet geming vebasait kee lat lag sakatee hain. adhyayan se pata chalata hai ki bachche jitana samay teevee, ghar / skool ke kampyootar aur geming par bitaate hain, usane bahut saaree chintaen badha dee hain. in samasyaon ke kaaran, bachchon ke jeevan mein shaamil gatividhiyon par maata-pita ke dekhabhaal karane kee avashyakata hai.

6. Ankita Sarkar

Ankita Sarkar is a girl from Jamshedpur. She did her graduation on Hospitality Management and now majoring in Child Psychology. She has published her own book and has been a part of many anthology books. She express her feelings through words.

Midnight Memories

Lying on my bed,
Looking at the sky,
Cool winds blowing through the night,
Like they are always by my side,
My mind wanders like a moon,
With the shooting stars and shimmery lights,
Which cuddles my memories with bright and calm,
The clouds which cover the moon
Is an armour to my memories,
The moon is calling me,
And saying,
It's a magical world with magical feelings.

7. Priya Das

She is Priya Das, passionate about writing and paintings. She is a trained artist, calligrapher and a published writer. She loves to play with beautiful words and is fond of reading books.Her writings portray a contrast of nature and a glimpse of reality of life .At present she is pursuing Bsc in Biotechnology.

Technology:

Technology is a boon or curse,
Depends on you, how it works.
It fulfilled all our necessity ,
But reduces the human working capacity.
Save our time and energy,
Technology has worked for us over century.
Connected people all over the world within a second.
Technology make it easy to learn a lesson.
The boon of technology is plenty.
Technology is a great human welfare achievement.
Use it wisely , to fulfill your requirement.

8. Mohammed Niyaz

Mohammed Niyaz hails from Mumbai - The City Of Dreams. He often loves to write poetries and short music video stories for his own youtube channel. Apart from this Mohammed is currently working on his upcoming anthologies, as well writing poetries since 2013. You can find him on facebook/mohammed niyaz as well on instagram @niyazsks..

Stage Of Troubles

Teeth falling from old to permanent.
Fear of losing all is the biggest incident.
From one to ten table exists in those minds.
Sickness of memory loss till they find.
Hopes that live with in alive.
For a moment when they are live.
Laughter is the best medicine.
Sadness behind tears of acne.
Pimples that never say goodbye.
Today or tomorrow face without shy.
Curiosity of career they think about.
Never gonna be ready to thought.
Missions of success is the dream.
Failures are co-members of the team.
Life is all about experiencing "stage of troubles".
At every single moment they might be getting doubles.

9. Srija Sadhukhan

Srija Sadhukhan is 19 years old girl studying BSc Biotechnology in Amity University Kolkata. Love to write poetry and a book worm too.

SOCIAL MEDIA

In this fast moving digital world
Everything just ends in double tap.
Everyone forget about the real heart
Actually giving heart in the digitalized one,
No one even takes a millisecond to appreciate
The efforts, credits and hardworking.
Social media got obsession with
Likes, comments, chats, followers and following.
But when there is no one to talk in social media
Then everyone realise how many are there in real life.
With whom having a real talk,
Though the social media and vicious cycle continues.

10. Jharna Upadhayay

She is Jharna Upadhayay. She is a beautiful writer from Assam. She is 17 years old. She started her writing from last 2 years. Apart from writing, she loves to read books (Novel's). She loves to read, buy and collect books. She can be called as Bibliophile. She has huge interest in singing, acting and sports. She also loves to write poems, quotes and stories. You can follow her on Yourquote.in.

ADDICTION TO MOBILE BY YOUNGSTERS

The use of mobile phones in present life is useful,but its addiction by present youngsters is dangerous.It threatens the very fabric of society. A study suggests, that majority of teenagers are fanatical about being always available and are extremely uneasy if unable to contact their friends.If the trend continues, young people will soon be incapable of forming and maintaining relationships without the help of a mobile, the study by leading Sociologists concludes. Youngsters are using their handset to send millions of text message to friends each day. Children want to be in so many groups and think that without a mobile they'll be in a river of unknown world.

It's also seen that the child from the age of 3 to 4 years to teenagers spend too much time in playing games on mobile. The mobile phone now often substitutes for physical play. The time spend on mobile is affecting other important activities such as recreational, reading and studying.Those aged between 16 and 20 prefer text messaging to all other means of written communication. A survey last year highlighted the increased risk to children under 16 using mobile and suggested that children below this age should be allowed to make calls only in emergencies.

Smartphones

What the hell !
Smartphone has made everyone enthral.
It's neither fake nor a lie,
Spectacles are seen on everyone's eye.
At shop, office ,home or sitting alone
No work done today in the absence of smart phone.
Youth, middle age or old
Look like they're watching mobile phones recklessly, with their brain sold!
Students grades are getting low,
At last they just say Oh! No,
Holding their teachers and parents toe,
Ensuring that they will enhance,
Just in flow..
Everyone has become smartphone's addict,
After realisation of time wasted on it,
Our mind say Oh! Shit..
Your cell phones has already replaced your watch,camera, calendar and alarm clock. Please don't let it replace your friends and family.

11. Miss Haquikat

Haquikat is an 18 year old creative girl with the bessings of words that's the most powerful weapon for her, haquikat writes hindi and urdu poetry article, gazal, nazm ,shayri etc she is the co author of 150+anthologies and currently she is compiling 6 Anthologies ,her 3 solo books are going to launch soon, haquikat wanna help peoples in finding their true self and real souls and happiness of life. Haquikat is a spiritual girl, she called her dad her first inspiration .she started writing in 11th standard and in just two years she wrote down many books and penned down thousands of beautiful and asthetic poetries,, she called herself a stubborn dreamer,, her pen is the statue of her temple of heart......

<<<WEB CAUGHT >>>

Web cought ....
Introvert extrovert me duniya bat gayi
Gale lagau kise yaha dooriyan chhat gaayi
Dilase ke naam pe ek imoji laga do
Kaun kiska kitna hai sab samjha do
Feelings to apna astitv hi mita gayi
Zindagi chhoti si screen me sama gayi
Tooti footi zindagi bhale
Likes aaye to zindagi chale
Social media ka mukhota pehenkar
Zindagi chhip gayi internet tale

Aksar main phone fod deti hu
Pinjra bas ek dimaag ka tod deti hoon
Mobile ki duniya me khoyi
Mood off se dosti hui
Dard dard ka ratta hai sab par
Aitbaar karu main kis kispar
Online offline me jajbaat simat gaye
Block karne bhar se rishte toot gaye
Koshish karti hu ye sab ko nazarandaaz kar saku
Khud se do pal sahi haske baat kar saku
Maathe ki shikan ko badha sa paati hu
Zindagi ko zamin pe gira sa pati hu
Koi emotional sa jaal hai ye
Haan main isme ulajh jati hu
...miss haquikat

12. Kavitha

Kavitha is a Maths graduate working as a System Engineer at Tata consultancy services in Bangalore. She is from Gobichettipalayam, Tamilnadu.She is a creative thinker, a Math lover, love to read books and write poems. Belives in the words " Future is not what we planned for tomorrow, it is the work what we do today..

Let internet be within limit

Internet is everywhere and is with everyone in their hands. It's is of affordable price and even sometimes we top up the package cutting other expenses as it has become as essential thing.

Everything is good only to a certain limit and it depends how we use the resource. Coming to the bad influence of the internet most of the people reduced thier physical activity and they waste their time simple searching, or watching or plying unnecessary things.

Adults are plying games or watching you tube videos which they doesn't need for thier well being.And some people who open accounts in the social media get addicted to it, that their will not pass without opening these applications once

Now a days children are well versed in using internet to the extend, they fight with their parents for separate gadgets. They doesn't know everything about it, when unwanted adds pop up they will open with the curiosity and finally ends in bigger problems.

There is no problem when it is just used as resource or a medium for geniune communication, when it goes beyond the limit then it is a curse for the society.

13. MURALIDHAR BANSAL

HE IS MURALIDHAR BANSAL FROM NEPAL. HE IS A BUSINESSMAN AT PRESENT. HE WAS INSPIRED TO WRITE AS A STUDENT SEEING THE ENVIRONMENT AROUND HIM. HE LOVES WRITING AS A HOBBY AND HE WANTS TO BE A GOOD AND RATIONAL BUSINSSSMAN.

INTERNET IS A MEDIUM TO REACH THE DESIRED PURPOSE AND THESE DAYS CHILDREN ARE SEEN ADDICTED TO IT RATHER THAN THE PURPOSE. CHILDREN ARE THE FUTURE OF THE NATION. THE USE OF INTERNET HAS BEEN MISUSED BY THE CHILDREN. A BIT NEGLIGENCE AND A BIT CARELESSNESS HAS BECOME A BURNING ISSUE.

THE MISUSE HAS BEEN INCREASING. THE EXPLICIT ACTIVITIES, ONLINE GAMES, ETC HAS HAMPERED THE GROWTH AND DEVELOPMENT OF THE CHILDREN. PERHAPS IN THE NAME OF STUDY, THE CHILDREN ARE DISGUISING THEMSELVES AND PARENTS, MOREOVER.

THIS SHOULD BE TAKEN CARE WITH AN IMMEDIATE EFFECT.

14. Aanushnaa Bandyopadhyay

Aanushnaa Bandyopadhyay is a girl from Kolkata, studying in St. Xavier's Institution, class 8. She loves showing her creativity through arts and wants to be a professional violinist and a great writer. She's currently the ambassador of Imprint Publication and the Founder of Inking Hearts Writing Community. She has worked as the compiler of three books, namely, "The Independent Pen", "The Saga of Love" and "Women, not Weak", among which two came in the top 100 bestselling books on Amazon. She had also been a co-author of 80+ anthologies and won many writing challenges held by various writing communities. @bandyopadhyay.aanushnaa_2020

ONE WENT MISSING

I headed towards the unknown house situated in the mid of the forest, that I had been seeing for a long line since my childhood whenever I passed through that place. But never did I saw anyone living there or coming out of that house! Out of curious and anxiety, one day I decided to visit that house once that we all feared.

From childhood, we had been hearing to the stories of a ghost, living in that house, so as it was our holiday, we planned to go there and stay there for few hours.

We reached there before having our breakfast, as we had plans to have meal there only. So we packed our lunches and snacks with us along.

The whole day was good. No disturbing, no horrific things, we were almost sure that all the rumours were fake, until it striked 5!

Suddenly, all the lights went off. We had candles with us, so we lighted them. But when we were busy with the darkness, one of your friend went missing! We got scared! We wanted to get out of this house, but couldn't find the door, it seemed that there was no door to went outside! All of a sudden, after sometime, our another two friends went missing, we felt more dead than alive!

Same went out for hours, until I was only left in the room, standing all alone! I didn't had any idea where they were going, then suddenly everyone screamed out, " Happy Birthday, Ana " I was so shocked that I could feel my heartbeat running 100 times faster! I felt relieved after knowing that they were pranking me to suprise me for my birthday. I looked at the clock, it was 12.

After cutting the cake, we were all set to return, when we realised that one of our friend was really missing, and no body knew where he was!

15. Rachana Saha

Rachana Saha, a budding writer. She has a great interest and love in writing. She bleeds her feelings in her diary. She is in class 8 reading in St. Xavier's Institution. She is born and brought up in Kolkata. She is co author of many anthologies and wants to write more. She is compiler of two books THE BLANK PAGE and BLEEDING METAPHOR. Other than writings, she has a great interest in drawing.

It was pill
Or maybe some kind of devilish magic
Either it was something
But still inside and outside was of me,
Just as the tree is covered with leaves
Below and above, Equally
Wayward; full of
Changes, loses and worth.
They asked the question of grief and happiness
Together what it means.
And it came to me,
All I could say; let me
Exhale this moment,
Release the burden I carried
And, let this next breathe be only mine.

16. Shubhanjali Nishad

Name of co author is shubhanjali nishad she completed his graduation in CSJM university she lives in Kanpur up her passion is writing nd she works as co author in 30+ antology books she loves writing becuase she knows very well writing is the best method to express your feelings through pen infornt of peoples she is the blessing of Krishna Ji she wrotes all the words by heart she tries to keep well writing in fornt of peoples becuase when she penned down in the paper she wrotes and decorates words with his soulfull and create own ideas and imagination..

-Right use of technologys gives you benfit nd worngs use of technologies is harmful for everyone
Aj k samay mein kitni sari nayi techeniques agyi hai jo ki hmare liye achi bhi hai toh kahi na kahi inka galt use harame liye bura bhi hai
Aksar hm chotte bachoo ko phones pkda dete hai pr na unhe dekhetey hai na guide krte hai kya wo kre hai hein galt hai ya sahi
Kyuki aj ka time esa hogya hai hme har waqt bachoo ko phones ineternet chlate waqt unpr dhyn dena cahahiye kya wo glt kre h kya sahi yh btana chahiye
Kyuki ajkl internet pr itni social sites agyi hai bachhe id bna kr chlana toh jante h pr unka sahi use nahi jante
Social sites hmare liye useful hai pr sirf padne likhne k liye kyuki ajkl internet pr itne games or kayi apss ese agye h jinki latt hmare ane wale bacho ko bigad rhi hai jo ki kl ka jaak is desh ka future banega

Aj k time yeh hogya h agr bacho ko phone na mile toh wo jaan tk de dete h y chori krte hai games na mile khelne ko to pagl hojate h

Aj k time phones or laptop dete waqt sb parents ki jimmedari hoti h unko dekhe or guide kre kya sahi h kya glt hai.

17. Anwesha Rath

Anwesha Rath,

A girl from small town used to see huge dreams now is working in anthologies is just 19 years old doing graduation her aim is just to take care of her parents as they cared for her till her dream is not writing poems but to share heartfelt message..

The good morning is known from whatsapp,
Your face seems to be bad .
To look beautiful you put filter ,
More like on facebook.
The more popular you look ,
The more followers in instagram .
Is known your standard
Telegram less for use more for chat
Hike for sticker,
And money for data charge
Day by day get more attracted
And more attached,
Opposite from your work get detached
So many website
So many people ,
Just for few likes, followers and enjoyment
Our life is in loss... artfelt message..

18. Pallavi Mehta

This is pallavi mehta. Writing is my passion. I am persuing graduation in the field of English literature. I have keen interest in creative writing, poetry, singing hymns...etc. I am co-author of many books even . I express my feelings in my writing. I have a firm belief that hard work and consistency will enable me to attain the impossible and make me strong enough to sparkle the lives of others.

Internet

Internet which simply moves data from one site to another, so that we can chat, browse and share. Everything is digitalize. But is it boon or bane for us??

The young generation mainly kids are highly impelled by internet. They are socially connected but mentally disturbed. Children indulge themselves into the cell playing online games, chatting and wasting their time in such innocency. Internet highly manipulate them . Internet helps us to feel close with our far friends and relatives. But is it happening? Their physical fitness seems to be vanish. It makes them indolent. Children are not enough wise to understand difference between good or bad. Major part of this age are trapped by proliferation of fake news such as cyber bullying , porn , sextortion,internate addiction and cohesion. They are going into depression. It establish inconvenience. Due to these , suicidal tendencies increases and they are suffering from anxiety and mentally harassed. Internet meant to be bane for new generation.

19. Zaira Shahid

I'm Zaira Shahid, a 19-year-old. Writing to give liberation to my tangled thoughts.

Their brains were then,
a blank canvas
ready to paint
the colors of life,
But now has this
deadly tech
cloged the lucid
minds of them,
Their aim now,
revolve by the fake target .
Their valued have gone
into dusty carpet,
They have no time
to groom the morals
They are just lost
in vicious quarells,
The net of this cyberspace
has rusted their blank
slate igniting the fire
"the war of hate"!

20. Hidden.Ethereal. Demoiselle

She is known by her pen name HIDDEN DEMOISELLE. She wants the world to know her by her words. She is a WALLFLOWER. She dwells in a mystical world created by her own imagination.

And how would people stranded within the internet ever fathom the harmonious melody?
All they could ever give in return are fake niceties!

21. Ishita Banerjee

Born in January 2003 in kolkata , West Bengal studied till class 12 at St. Pauls boarding and day school, Kolkata.Currently pursuing BBA(Hospital Management) in NSHM Knowledge Campus, Kolkata . She has been writing poems ever since she was in class 6.Some of her works has also have been published in some local newspapers like The Telegraph(TTIS) and school magazines.Her poems have been featured in the book THE LAST FLOWER OF SPRING by Poem Pajama publications under Delhi Poerty Slam. "WHISPER OF HEARTS" by Bookfever publications and " MIRAKEE " by TGIWC.She also wants to write more in future and inspire all the sections of the society.

Social Media Disruption

Food was ordered ages passed
I forgot when I had eaten warm food last
Her follower gets to see our food
Before we even get to eat
I have learnt the menu card it's still the same, no matter how many times I read
Click and post
There goes cold the chicken roast
This is how my appetite is mostly lost
But I still have to smile and bear the entire cost.

22. Srishti Morya

Myself Srishti Morya belongs to Faridabad, Haryana. My Parents name is Mr. Pankaj Kumar and Mrs. Madhuri Morya. I'm studying Journalism and also an NSS Volunteer. I love to write Quote, Letter to the Editor, Poem and Fictional Story. My Letter to the Editor published in various newspapers and also published poem in a college magazine. I'm very creative and an imaginary girl. I have worked as a co-author in 130+ Anthology and I am also a compiler of own anthology "OUR CHILDHOOD" , "THE DREAM WORLD", "SKY LANTERNS: CLOSE TO HEART " , "WIND CHIMES" , "FEAR: TO LOST SOMEONE IN LIFE" And "PRINCESS IN THE MAGICAL WORLD". My solo book will be published soon "HUMARI JEEVAN KI ATRANGI DUNIYA".

Badhta internet ka aser aaj kal ke bacho pr bhaut bura prabhav hai. Agar hum ise nazarandaaz karna chahe to bhi nahi kr skte. Kam age ke bacche aaj kl phone ke peeche ladai krte hai parantu ye bhaut hi galat hai. Aaj ke samay ese ese news aate hai jisme internet ko ab chote baccho ke saath jod diya ho.

Bad influence of internet mentally bahut effect krta hai, jha se unhe career ki shuruaat krna hota hai waha pr bacche internet ke peeche apne career kharab kr dete hai. Es cheej ko sochna chahiye naa sirf hm apni zindagi balki hm apna time in galat cheejo pr lgakar waste kr rahe hai ye galat baat hai.

23. Ankita Pandey

Being a strong headed person Ankita Pandey is a CS in making. She started having an interest in graphic designing from the age of 14 and in future has plans to follow her passion. She started writing from the age of 16 and still feel refreshing to express herself to her diary.

She feels content when her video edits and writeups are being appreciated and encourage her to work more enthusiastically. She has by far did wonders in video edits and photoshop skills. She is surely making a good impact by her writing talent too.

Good morning smiling city.
Good morning smiling city,
What a beautiful morning.
Welcome every morning with a smile.
Sun is looking at everyone with a smile.
And sending rays of happiness.
Beautiful birds are singing,
Kids are dancing.
Good morning smiling city,
Everyone starts their new day and leaves their nightmares.
God wants us to do a new thing in life.
The new day brings new hope.
Many new opportunities are waiting for you.
Good morning smiling city,
Some people are waiting for the bus.

It looks beautiful to sit inside a bus,
And see a city from the windows.
Children's are getting ready to get one step closer to their careers.
Good morning smiling city,
There will be so much beauty you will find in the morning.
In the night we end our day and start dreaming.
And the next day we make plans to complete it.

24. Zeenat

I am Zeenat. I am 16 years of age. I am currently a school student of class 11th. Writing is my hobby, my passion. And I want to be a worldwide writer. I have participated in many anthologies and also in open mics. I am currently working on my solo novel.

The Internet.

Internet made so easy
Ease our lives
Internet give us benefits
Avail us for the needs.
Behind this, there is something
Something very bad
A second face of internet
For the country, that is so sad
Internet make us connect
Connect to the people
But now making us away
Away from the real ones.
Internet give us information
That is right in proper way
"How to make poison from the apple seeds"
so, about this info what will u say
Internet provide entertainment
Watching our favourites at any time
Enjoy the sexual things
Is a natural crime.

Internet make us employed
For our livelihoods
Hacking someone's bank account
Isn't it enough good.
Today,
Internet makes everything easy
But to apply this ease in a positive way
I really a big question
That makes everyone sleazy..

25. Sabrin Sultan

Assalamualaikum Everyone! The name of this coauthor is Sabrin Sultan. She is a girl who prefers reading The Quran as her favourite book above anything else. She loves writing and in school, her notebooks were always full of scribbles.

She has her love for writing from her fellows who always encouraged her to keep penning down her thoughts. She believes that Writing is her way of coping with all of her emotions and a way to reach out to people when other words fall short.

Internet

Internet, internet
In every cell phone it is set
All the world I have been Adults are always busy scrolling the screen
Using the internet has been fashion. Transforming studies online has been a passion.
Internet can be useful
To sharpen the mind it is an important tool
using internet makes us cool
Life without the internet can make one fool.
The Internet is popular all over the world's colleges and schools.
Using the internet is like following a vital rule.
Sometimes using internet can harm
Severely we can feel the pain in our arm.
Sometimes using the internet can be a waste of time

Instead of wasting time, it is better to drink a glass of lime.
The Internet is a brain teaser which teases
Oh! users please be careful your brain power can freeze.
Lot of time can be wasted in chit chatting
Instead of batting it is better to watch Sachin's batting
Internet separates you from having ones
And by using internet it gets lot of fun
It rots the sense in the head
It stops and kills the imagination road
The most important thing we have learned
almost everyone has been concerned
Oh! users please never use internet
Instead of the internet, give them a loving pet!
News and events all over the world can be shared by internet just by installing a data pack
Oh! users don't worry 2G, 3G, 4G
are available in no of second
Internet is costume tied around your neck
If a virus destroys your internet you cannot remake.

26. Sniawshngain Joseph Papang

He is Sniawshngain Joseph Papang, who wanna travel all the universe with his thoughts and ideas through his sword called Pen; and give light to those who are in the dark. He is from a simple village of Rtiang, Meghalaya- Shillong. He likes reading and writing is his passion. He is a writer, poet. He has co-authored 15 plus Anthologies and he is still working on many more at present. Currently, he is a student of BTech at Assam Don Bosco University, Guwahati, Azara.

Connection Lost

Have you ever wondered how dependent are we on gadgets and media? They are everywhere, are used for almost everything, and are seamlessly integrated into our lives- from the time we wake up till we fall asleep. But suddenly, the electricity goes out, and they all shut down- the internet, televisions, desktops, microwaves, fridges, lights, fans, and countless other things.

It is as a major part of our life is in a blackout.

All is not lost if we are lucky that our Laptops and Cell Phones have some charge left. However, at any point, they eventually shut down, and we feel like fish out of water. There is nothing to do, nothing to listen to, to watch, and no way to peek into the digital world.

We feel restless, breathless and confused. We feel like we are missing out on something

This leads me to reflect: Are we dependent only on Gadgets and Media for our daily living?

Can we stay a while without these things?

Do internets affect my daily lives- family, study and others?

Am I a slave of these things?

Do I able to be the master and use to build my society through media?

You can raise lots and tones of questions and am not going to give any answer.

We are all aware of these things and let's answer for ourselves.

27. Mohd Mohsin Khan

Mohd Mohsin Khan from Lucknow, is currently a student pursuing his BTech from Vellore Institute of Technology, Bhopal. He is a writer by day and a reader by night. He personally believes that, by writing we can express our feelings in a more efficient and easy way. He further says that writing is a passion which is ignited by thoughts and that is fluid by ink. It's a way to travel through someone's mind, leaving us with smiles for miles, depending on which route we go. You can contact him on Insta- @_archaic_rhymist or Email him on- 786mohsin0khan@gmail.com

Stuck in hect.

Throw your phone,
Photos captured at,
Everything online isn't real,
Evict the tutor from your home,
The absolute worst day,
Phone is a pretty evil place,
Facebook, Instagram, Twitter,
Are really the same,
Without living, we actually click,
Connecting people, with fake face,
True or not,
People put something everyday,
Morning, take a second to reminisce,

Phone on my side, is the first I go for,
I plugged, I rebooted, I reset,
And all I realised is I am stuck all over,
Yeah, a life stuck,
In a bad influence of you.

28. Pranav Kumar

Mera nam Pranav kumar hai,mai Bihar me Khagaria jile ke Rahimpur , panchkutti gaaw me rahta hu. Mujhe pachpan se hi likhne ka aur kavita likhna psand hai sath me mujhe khel me volleyball khelna pasand hai .

Internet ka bura prabhav chhote bachcho par kya ho rha hai..

Aaj ke samay me hamara jeewan bahut see cheej par nirbhar karta hai. Agar wah cheej hamare jeewan me nahi rahta to aaj hamara jeewan itna aasan nahi rahta. jaise agar upkaran nahi aata to hamare jeewan ka har kary ko karne me muskil aatee. Isee cheej me ek cheej hai internet jisko ham hindi me karyjal kahte hai aaj ke samay me pooree duniya internet par hee jada tar nirbhar hai.jaise har kam internet par hee ho rhee hai. Hospital , polish station, railway station se lekar bre–bre factory company or shiksha ke kshetra me bhee internet ka upyog ho rha hai. Din par din internet ka upyog ish duniya me badhta hee ja rha hai, ish karan se internet ka bura prabhaw chhote bachcho par ho rha hai. Yah prabhaw bachcho par ush karan ho rha hai, kee mata ,pita ya ghar ke bre bachcho ke sath sab milkar baith kar pahle jwane kee trah bate nahi karte hai.or sab apne kam me itna kho jate hai ,kee bachcho ke liye samay bhee nahi nikal pate hai, ish karan bachche phone lekar usme internet ke jriye free fire jaise internet game khelte hai,or dheere–dheere bache iske aadheen ho jate hai.or iske sath bachche social media jaise instagram, Facebook, tik tok,ityadu app phone me download kar ke use achchhi bat nahi seekh kar galat bat seekhne lagte hai or mata ,pita bhi bachcho ko ishme brabha dete hai aap sab soch rhe honge kya mata–pita ishme kis tarah samil ho gye jo apne hee bachche ko galat rah par laye to me bta dena chahta hu,kee agar kisee ka bachcha khana nahi khaya ya rooth jaye to use mnane ke liye ham sab oose phone de dete hai ,or ham apne kam me wyast ho jate hai.or sochte hai kya ab bachcha shant ho gya hai,thore der baad phone chhor dega lekin yhee kam ham apne bachcho ko internet kee aadat lgate hai. Yhee internet kee aadat bachcho ko buree cheej sikhatee hai ,or internet ka bura prabhaw bachcho par hota hai.or agar samay rahte ispar mata–pita ka dhyan nhi jaye to wah bachche log dipration ka shikar ho jate hai or aatamhitya kar lete hai. Isliye me sbhee mata–pita se bintee karta hu,kee aap apne bachcho ke liye kuchh samay nikal kar uskee man kee bat ko suniye or use bate kriye or sath me ek or bintee mai aap sbhee se karta hu agar kisee mata–pita ka bachcha rooth jaye to phone dene ke badle oose mnaee or jada rooth jaye to khilauna dilane ka wada kriye. Chliye isee ke sath me apne lekhak ko yhee samapt karta hu dhanyabad.

29. Khyati Sahrawat

Khyati Sahrawat is a 15-year-old girl who advocates change and self discovery. She stays open to learning and wishes to widen her horizon of thinking.

Social media influencers, celebrities and most of the people we look up to attest to the fact that they are or have been familiar with the feeling of not being good enough. YouTubers talk about how gaining their first

1000 subscribers felt more fulfilling than 1 million. The more we accomplish the more our goals expand, the more the insatiability of human beings illuminates itself. But ascending our goals and desires is rarely about self-actualisation and working in accordance with our potentialities once we realise them rather it is more about dissatisfaction, majorly about not feeling 'enough'. There is a thin yet fine line between self actualisation and dissatisfaction. Self actualisation is a healthy way of directing our efforts to accomplish bigger goals, it's about knowing that you are good enough, all that you do is solely because YOU want to do it, because it means something to YOU, all that you need to accomplish something is within you, the means rest within you because you are enough, it's about appreciating your present, acknowledging your past, working towards your future while being satisfied with your presence, it's about breaking your own limits, outgrowing yourself and evolving because it is significant for you. On the contrary chronic dissatisfaction is a byproduct of comparison. Comparison is the thief of all joy, we compare our struggles to someone else's highlights, someone else's success doesn't indicate failure, anything less than out dream job is not failure. Chronic dissatisfaction makes us look outward with envy and inwards with disappointment.

Perhaps the only antidote to dissatisfaction is gratitude, redefining success, redefining 'enough'. Mariane Williamson wrote, "in our natural state we are glorious beings… our jailer is a three headed monster; one head our past, one our insecurities and one our popular culture." We need not comply with the indignations which are imposed upon us by the society, our definition of success need not be equivalent to someone else's because for some you won't ever be good enough but for some you will be worth it even when you are not at your best. The concepts of contentment and satisfaction are endlessly glorified by us but we clampdown the idea by subjectively defining success and making someone feel not enough simply because their achievements do not qualify the bar that is set for them, thereby, deterring individual happiness. Thus, happiness, contentment and satisfaction are an inside job meant for pleasing ourselves and not someone else because from societal perspectives we might just never be good enough.

30. Sarfaraz Ansari

I am Sarfaraz Ansari, I have completed graduation recent year, I am very fond of gaming, professionally I am a web developer now, and I am also interested in writing , and also taken parts in anthologies.

Internet

Nowadays people can quickly post anything on the internet and comment on different issues freely.

They consider the online world as a necessary part of their daily life.

Social networking is an amazing technological phenomenon of the 21st century. Social networking websites allow each user to create and design a personal website, using graphics, color, music, pictures and give it a unique character. This activity is particularly popular among young people and does not require specific technical knowledge. On these websites, users through their virtual profile work interactively with other users, publishing photos and videos, join groups of common interests, publish and exchange their artistic creations, visit pages of other users and use a variety of applications.

The Internet is a powerful tool in our hands, but if it is not used properly can put someone in a very risky situation. The challenge of the Internet is to be able to recognize potential hazards, to know how to prevent the risks and create options to avoid and terminate them.

The most significant problems that may be found in the social networking sites are:

Many people in this modern era would be in favor of freedom of speech, but it can harm people too.

- Freedom of speech for one guy can be an interference in the human right of another guy.
- For example, someone posts something on the internet following the freedom of speech, but it may be against someone else, in this way it is against human rights also.

Even a single word that you posted anywhere online can inflict a lot of people.

- There are various kinds of negative messages online too. Many of them are anonymous.
- People also use wrong words to comment on people without any reason. This is regarded as a cyberbully. Current cyberbully statistics show 69% of people admit to abusive online behavior.
- This can psychologically harm others.
- People most often lose hope when they are attacked by the negative comments of people online especially on social media.

The End

9 798887 726113

Printed by Libri Plureos GmbH in Hamburg, Germany